Crafts for Kids Who Are Wild About

Dinosaurs

Crafts for Kids Who Are

WILD

ABOUT

DINOSAURS

By Kathy Ross

Illustrated by Sharon Lane Holm

The Millbrook Press
Brookfield, Connecticut

For my daughter and my friend, Allison—K.R.
For my mother—S.L.H.

Library of Congress Cataloging-in-Publication Data
Ross, Kathy (Katharine Reynolds), 1948–
Crafts for kids who are wild about dinosaurs / Kathy Ross : illustrated by
Sharon Lane Holm.
p. cm.
Summary: Provides instructions for twenty projects, including a
triceratops ring-toss game, diplodocus body puppet, plesiosaur window
decoration, necktie tree, and dinosaur feet.
ISBN 0-7613-0053-8 (lib. bdg.) ISBN 0-7613-0177-1 (pbk.)
1. Handicraft—Juvenile literature. 2. Dinosaurs in art—Juvenile literature.
[1. Handicraft. 2. Dinosaurs in art.] I. Holm, Sharon Lane. II. Title
TT160.R71422   1997
745.5—dc20   96-14304   CIP   AC

Published by The Millbrook Press, Inc.
2 Old New Milford Road
Brookfield, Connecticut 06804

Contents

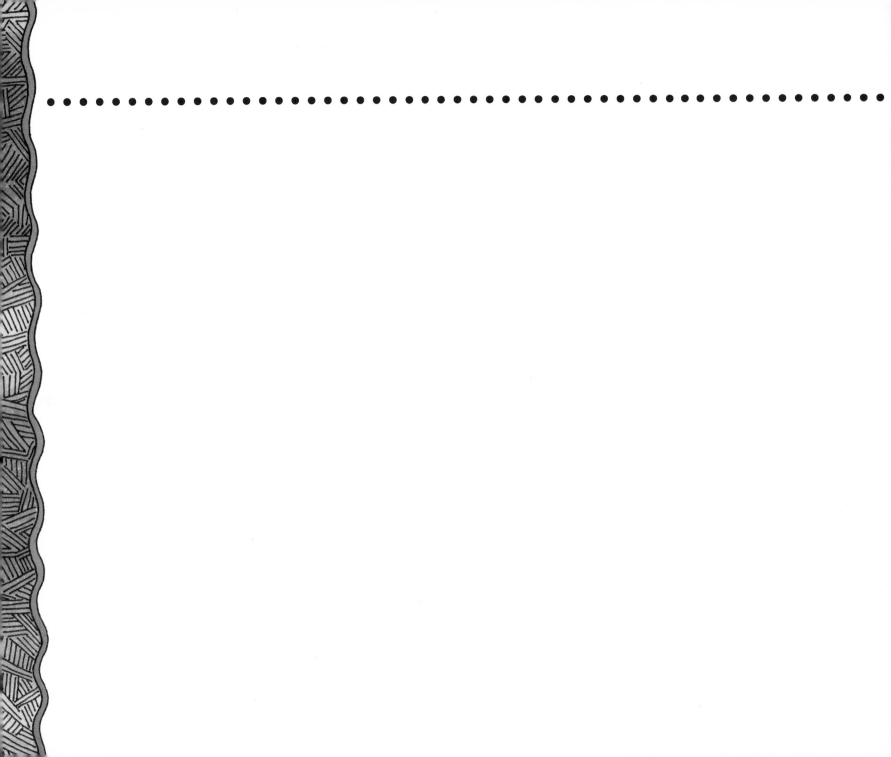

If you are learning about dinosaurs or are already fascinated by them, this is the book for you. It contains twenty projects related to dinosaurs and other animals from prehistoric times.

The special features of each of these creatures distinguish one kind from another. The projects patterned after actual dinosaurs will take more time and effort to make than some of the other projects—such as the plants.

When a project needs to be painted, I have not suggested a color because no one knows what color the dinosaurs were. You can decide for yourself the color or colors you will use.

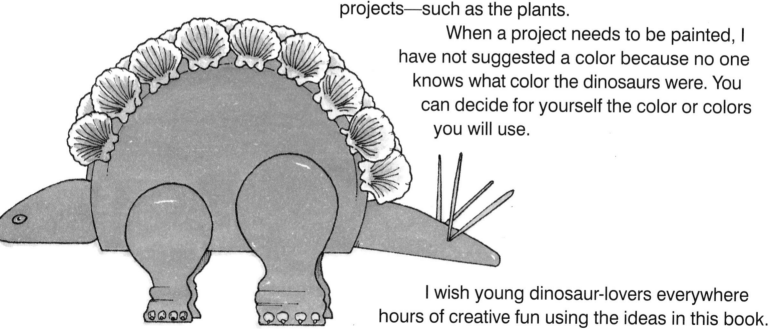

I wish young dinosaur-lovers everywhere hours of creative fun using the ideas in this book.

Pasta Fossil Plaque

Here is what you need:

potting soil
white glue
pasta in different shapes
Styrofoam tray
bowl and spoon
measuring cup
scissors
felt

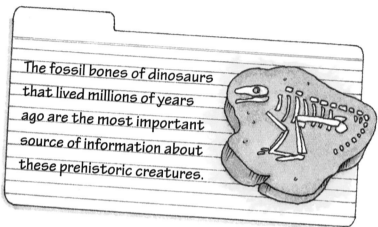

The fossil bones of dinosaurs that lived millions of years ago are the most important source of information about these prehistoric creatures.

Here is what you do:

Mix one cup of potting soil with just enough white glue to hold the dirt together. Shape the dirt into a ball and set it on the Styrofoam tray. Press the ball down until it is flat and about ½ inch (1.5 centimeters) thick.

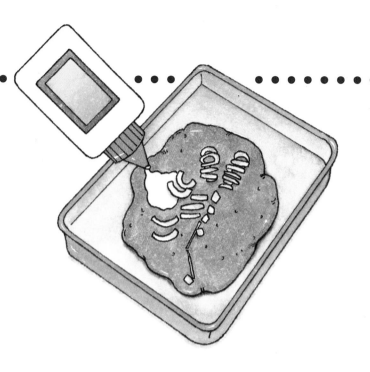

Pasta shapes make great "bones."
Arrange different pasta shapes to design your own fossil—the possibilities are endless! When you have a design you like, carefully arrange it on top of the gluey dirt. Gently press the pasta into the dirt to make sure it will stay. Cover the pasta with a layer of glue. Let the dirt dry on the Styrofoam tray until it is hard. This could take two or three days.

When the dirt is dry, cut a piece of felt to fit the bottom of the plaque. Glue the felt on the bottom of the dirt plaque to keep the plaque from scratching the surface you place it on.

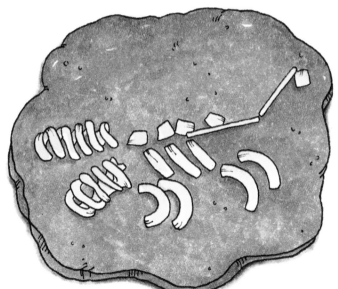

Make a fossil plaque for someone you know who is wild about dinosaurs.

Giant Apatosaurus Model

Here is what you need:

large oatmeal box with lid
six cardboard paper-towel tubes
two cardboard toilet-tissue tubes
two apple seeds
sharp, black permanent marker
sixteen elbow macaroni
large mixing bowl and spoon
measuring cup
white glue
scissors
old, dark-colored T-shirt
large Styrofoam or plastic-covered tray
cellophane tape

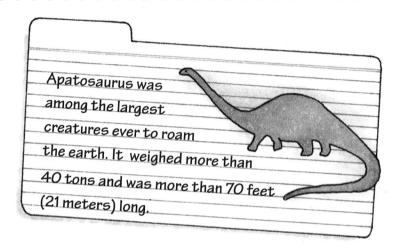

Apatosaurus was among the largest creatures ever to roam the earth. It weighed more than 40 tons and was more than 70 feet (21 meters) long.

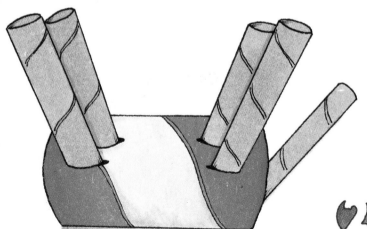

Here is what you do:

Turn the oatmeal box on its side. This will be the body of the dinosaur. To make the legs, draw four circles on the underside of the body, two at each end. Use the end of one of the paper-towel tubes as a pattern. Cut inside the traced circle so that the legs will be a tight fit. Insert a paper-towel tube into each of the four holes. If the hole is too small to get the tube through, just keep trimming small pieces from the edge of the hole until the tube fits.

To make the tail, cut a hole in the back of the dinosaur (one of the flat ends of the oatmeal box). Slide a paper-towel tube in the hole at an angle so that it points downward, just like a tail.

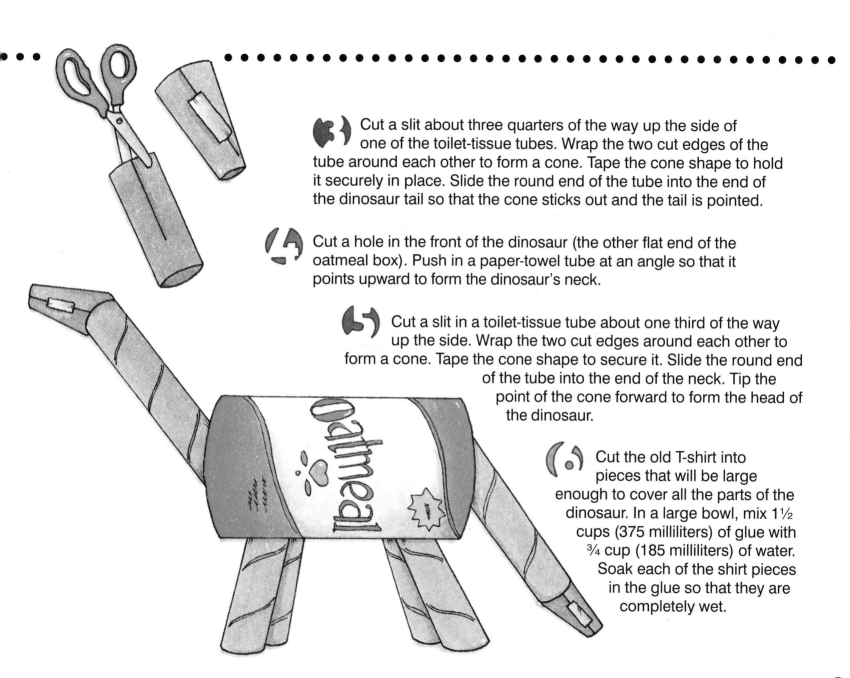

3 Cut a slit about three quarters of the way up the side of one of the toilet-tissue tubes. Wrap the two cut edges of the tube around each other to form a cone. Tape the cone shape to hold it securely in place. Slide the round end of the tube into the end of the dinosaur tail so that the cone sticks out and the tail is pointed.

4 Cut a hole in the front of the dinosaur (the other flat end of the oatmeal box). Push in a paper-towel tube at an angle so that it points upward to form the dinosaur's neck.

5 Cut a slit in a toilet-tissue tube about one third of the way up the side. Wrap the two cut edges around each other to form a cone. Tape the cone shape to secure it. Slide the round end of the tube into the end of the neck. Tip the point of the cone forward to form the head of the dinosaur.

6 Cut the old T-shirt into pieces that will be large enough to cover all the parts of the dinosaur. In a large bowl, mix 1½ cups (375 milliliters) of glue with ¾ cup (185 milliliters) of water. Soak each of the shirt pieces in the glue so that they are completely wet.

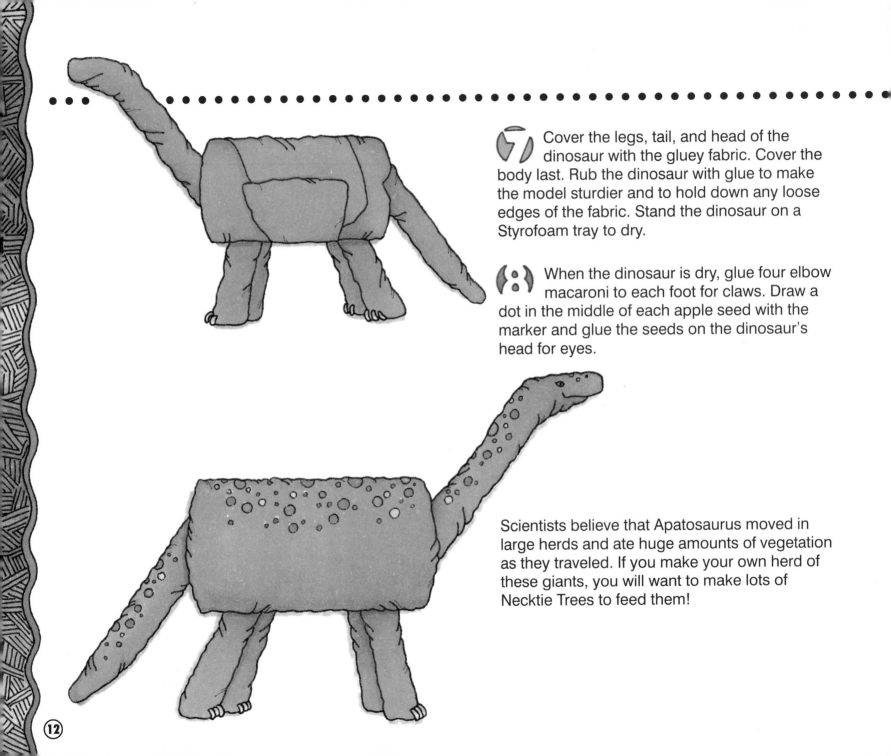

7 Cover the legs, tail, and head of the dinosaur with the gluey fabric. Cover the body last. Rub the dinosaur with glue to make the model sturdier and to hold down any loose edges of the fabric. Stand the dinosaur on a Styrofoam tray to dry.

8 When the dinosaur is dry, glue four elbow macaroni to each foot for claws. Draw a dot in the middle of each apple seed with the marker and glue the seeds on the dinosaur's head for eyes.

Scientists believe that Apatosaurus moved in large herds and ate huge amounts of vegetation as they traveled. If you make your own herd of these giants, you will want to make lots of Necktie Trees to feed them!

Necktie Tree

Here is what you need:

long cardboard wrapping-paper tube, about 2 inches
   (5 centimeters) in diameter
masking tape
twelve old neckties
scissors
white glue
paintbrush and green and brown poster paint
newspaper to work on

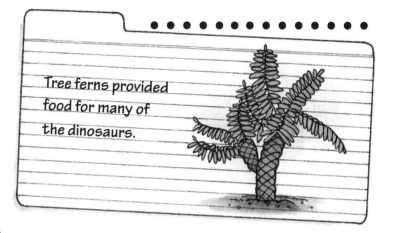

Tree ferns provided food for many of the dinosaurs.

Here is what you do:

1. Cut the tube so that it is about 22 inches (55 centimeters) long. Cover the outside of the tube in a random pattern with pieces of masking tape that are 1 inch (2.5 centimeters) square. It is easiest to tear off a long strip of tape first and then tear the smaller pieces off that strip. The tape will give the tube a rough, scaly look, like the bark of a tree.

2. Paint the tree trunk brown and let it dry.

3. Cut a piece 10 inches (25 centimeters) long from the thin end of each necktie. Rub glue around the top inside edge of the tree trunk and tuck the cut ends of the tie pieces into the top of the tree. Arrange the tie leaves so that they drape around the top of the tree.

4. Paint the leaves green and let them dry.

Stand one or more of these trees
near a hungry plant-eating dinosaur.

Plate Stegosaurus

Here is what you need:

three heavy 10-inch (25.4-centimeter) paper plates
eighteen or more medium-size seashells
sixteen popcorn kernels
two apple seeds
sharp, black permanent marker
four toothpicks
blue glue gel
paint brush and poster paints in colors of your choice
large Styrofoam tray

The Stegosaurus is best known for the plates that run down its back. Some scientists think the plates helped to control the body temperature of the dinosaur. Others think the plates protected the dinosaur's body.

Here is what you do:

Cut off one third of two of the paper plates. Cut legs for the dinosaur from the third plate. Be sure that the curved edge of the plate forms the feet. Cut a pointed tail and a small head from the flat portion of the scrap pieces of the first two plates.

Glue the two plates together, with the tops of the plates facing each other. Insert the dinosaur's head between the plates at one end and insert the tail at the opposite end. Glue the legs on the outsides of the plates, two on each side of the dinosaur.

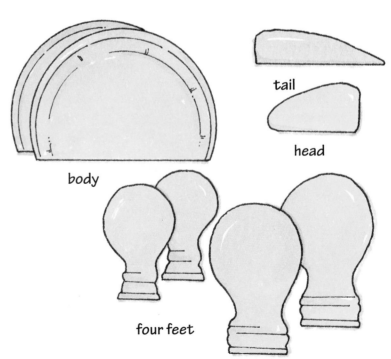

body

tail

head

four feet

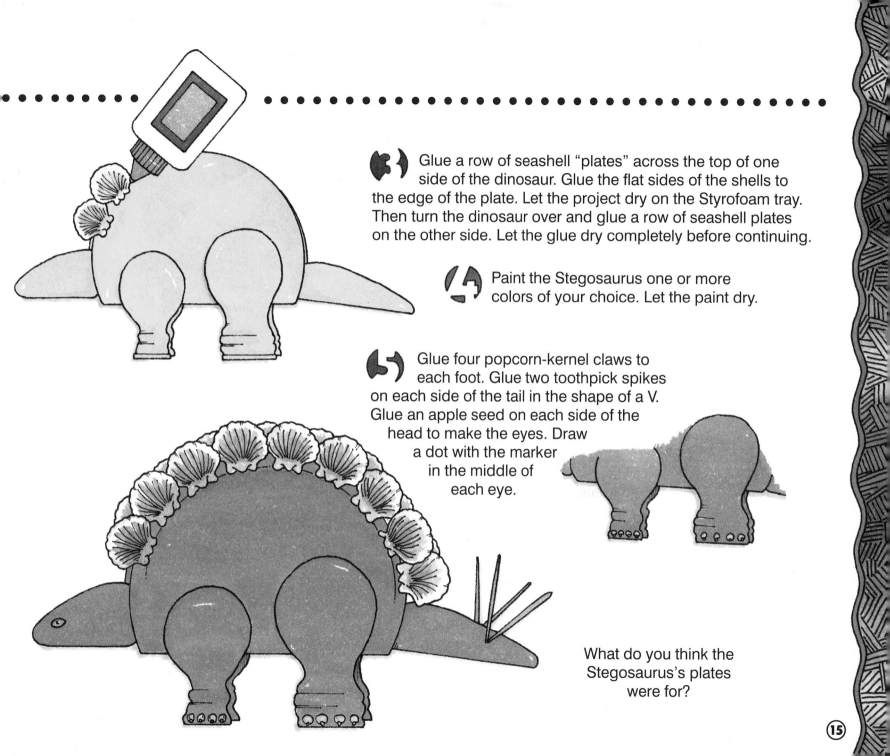

Glue a row of seashell "plates" across the top of one side of the dinosaur. Glue the flat sides of the shells to the edge of the plate. Let the project dry on the Styrofoam tray. Then turn the dinosaur over and glue a row of seashell plates on the other side. Let the glue dry completely before continuing.

Paint the Stegosaurus one or more colors of your choice. Let the paint dry.

Glue four popcorn-kernel claws to each foot. Glue two toothpick spikes on each side of the tail in the shape of a V. Glue an apple seed on each side of the head to make the eyes. Draw a dot with the marker in the middle of each eye.

What do you think the Stegosaurus's plates were for?

Triceratops Ring-Toss Game

Here is what you need:

eight 9-inch-diameter (23-centimeter) paper plates
stapler and staples
masking tape
scissors
paint brush and poster paint in colors of your choice
yellow scrap paper
black marker
blue glue gel
three 3-inch-diameter (7.6-centimeter) paper or plastic cups
hole punch
yarn
newspaper to work on

The Triceratops is best known for the three horns on its face—two above the eyes and one on the nose. This dinosaur also has a neck frill, a bony collar around the head. Scientists think this strong collar protected the animal's neck.

Here is what you do:

Overlap the halves of two paper plates, bottoms facing up. Staple the edges of the plates together. Staple the edge of another plate under each side of the first two plates to form a flower shape. You now have four plates stapled together.

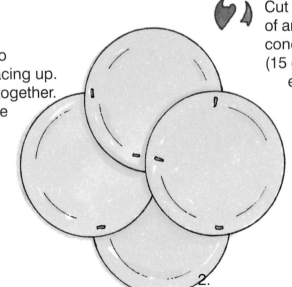

2.

Cut a slit from the edge to the center of another plate. Wrap the plate into a cone that has an opening about 6 inches (15 centimeters) wide. Staple the wrapped edges of the cone together to hold them in place. Cut a triangle-shaped piece out of the tip of the cone to make a mouth opening.

Staple the cone to the edge of one of the plates in the flower cluster. Staple another plate to the center of the cluster— it should overlap the bottom of the cone.

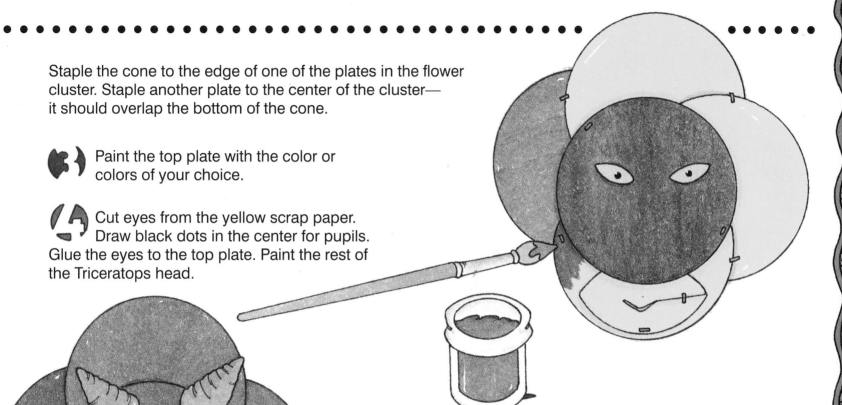

3 Paint the top plate with the color or colors of your choice.

4 Cut eyes from the yellow scrap paper. Draw black dots in the center for pupils. Glue the eyes to the top plate. Paint the rest of the Triceratops head.

5 To make two large horns, cut a plate in half. Fold each half of the plate into a cone and staple the edges to hold them in place. Wrap each cone with masking tape. Glue a horn above each eye.

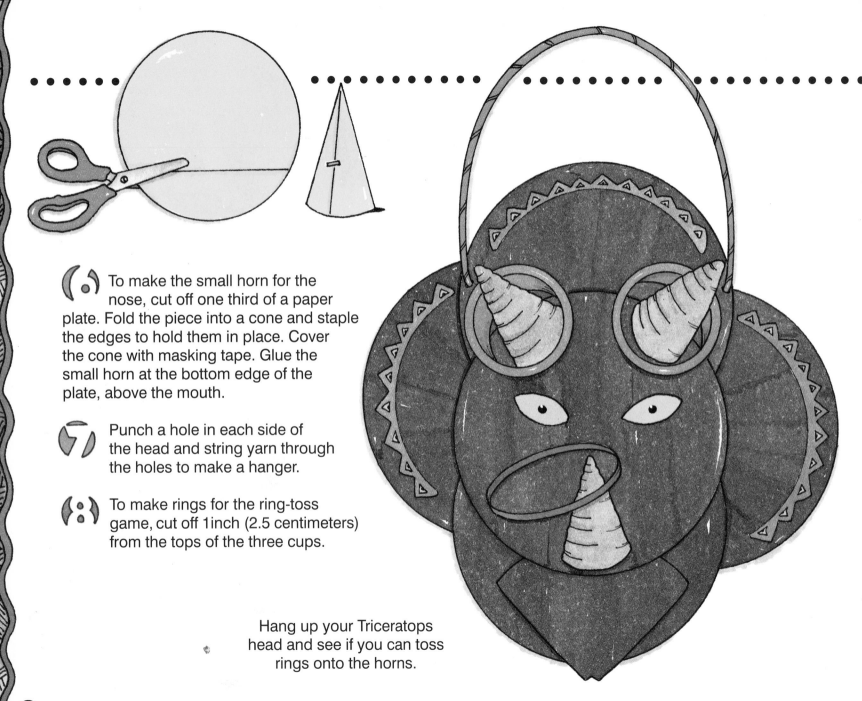

To make the small horn for the nose, cut off one third of a paper plate. Fold the piece into a cone and staple the edges to hold them in place. Cover the cone with masking tape. Glue the small horn at the bottom edge of the plate, above the mouth.

Punch a hole in each side of the head and string yarn through the holes to make a hanger.

To make rings for the ring-toss game, cut off 1 inch (2.5 centimeters) from the tops of the three cups.

Hang up your Triceratops head and see if you can toss rings onto the horns.

Early Flowering Plant

Here is what you need:

paper lunch bag
net produce bag, such as an onion bag
masking tape
white and yellow tissue paper
paintbrush and brown and green poster paint
scissors
newspaper for stuffing and to work on
Styrofoam tray

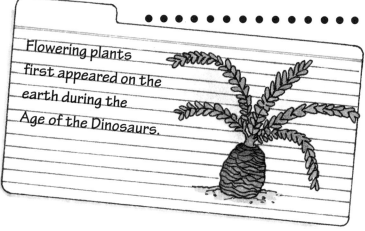

Flowering plants first appeared on the earth during the Age of the Dinosaurs.

Here is what you do:

1 Crumple some newspaper and stuff the lunch bag half full. Cover the stuffed part of the bag with the net bag. Wrap masking tape tightly around the bag and the netting just above the stuffing, about 3 inches (7.6 centimeters) from the top of the bag.

2 Cut the extra paper above the tape into four parts to form leaves at the top of the plant.

3 Paint the bottom of the net-covered bag with brown paint to make the bark of the plant. Paint the leaves at the top green. Place the bag on the Styrofoam tray and let the paint dry.

4 Cut flowers from the white tissue paper. Crumple bits of yellow tissue and glue one of the crumpled pieces in the center of each flower. Glue the flowers on the bark of the plant.

You can use a grocery bag instead of a lunch bag to make a larger version of this ancient plant.

Parasaurolophus Mask

Here is what you need:

12-inch by 14-inch (30-centimeter by 36-centimeter)
    poster board in color of your choice
tissue paper of same color as poster board
cardboard wrapping-paper tube, about 1 inch
    (2.5 centimeters) in diameter
paper party horn
masking tape
white glue
scissors
bowl
pencil
hole punch
string
newspaper to work on
Styrofoam trays

The Parasaurolophus had a long crest along the top of its head. Some scientists believe that the dinosaur blew air through the hollow bone of the crest and made a noise as a way to call other Parasaurolophuses.

Here is what you do:

1 Overlap the two bottom corners of the narrow side of the poster board to form a cone, leaving an opening at the end. Tape the overlapping edges together. Hold the poster board in front of your face like a mask, with your chin firmly in the cone-shaped end. On the front of the mask, gently mark in pencil where you should cut the eye holes. Remove the mask from your face, and cut out the eye holes with a scissors.

2 Cut the cardboard tube so that it is 20 inches (51 centimeters) long. Glue the tube along the center of the mask, between the eye holes, to make the crest. Use some masking tape to hold it in place while the glue is drying.

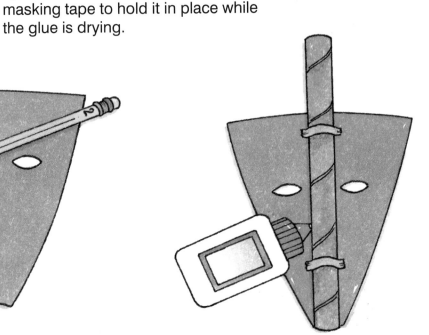

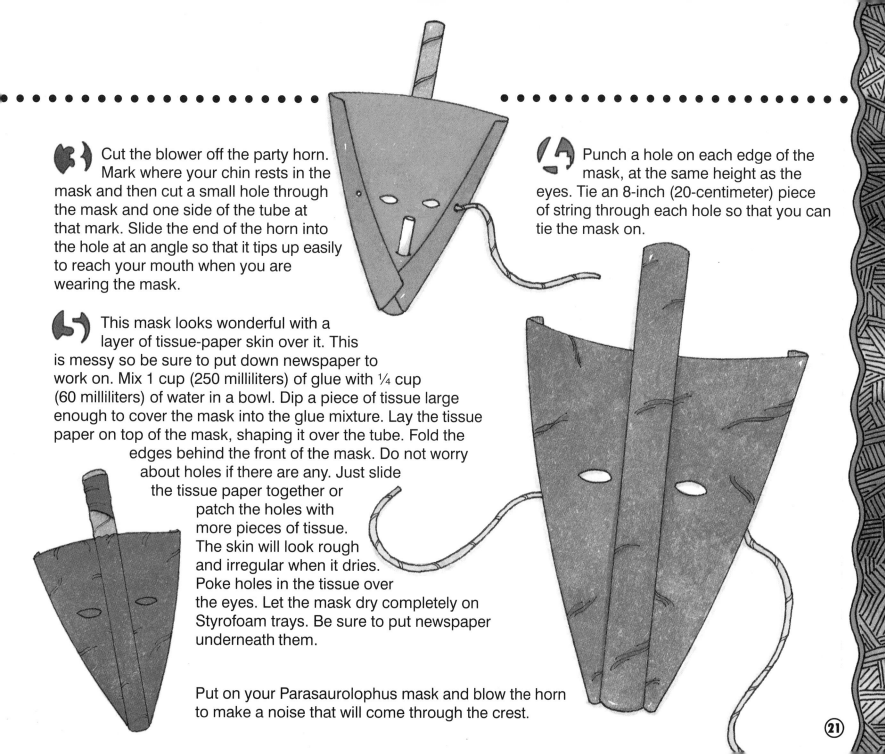

3 Cut the blower off the party horn. Mark where your chin rests in the mask and then cut a small hole through the mask and one side of the tube at that mark. Slide the end of the horn into the hole at an angle so that it tips up easily to reach your mouth when you are wearing the mask.

5 This mask looks wonderful with a layer of tissue-paper skin over it. This is messy so be sure to put down newspaper to work on. Mix 1 cup (250 milliliters) of glue with ¼ cup (60 milliliters) of water in a bowl. Dip a piece of tissue large enough to cover the mask into the glue mixture. Lay the tissue paper on top of the mask, shaping it over the tube. Fold the edges behind the front of the mask. Do not worry about holes if there are any. Just slide the tissue paper together or patch the holes with more pieces of tissue. The skin will look rough and irregular when it dries. Poke holes in the tissue over the eyes. Let the mask dry completely on Styrofoam trays. Be sure to put newspaper underneath them.

Put on your Parasaurolophus mask and blow the horn to make a noise that will come through the crest.

4 Punch a hole on each edge of the mask, at the same height as the eyes. Tie an 8-inch (20-centimeter) piece of string through each hole so that you can tie the mask on.

Hatching Troodon Puppet

Here is what you need:

large oatmeal box
2-inch (5-centimeter) Styrofoam ball
two flat wooden ice-cream spoons
two cat's-eye marbles
aluminum foil
dark-colored, adult-size sock
15-inch (38-centimeter) stick or dowel
masking tape
scissors
white glue

The Troodon had a birdlike head and very large eyes, which scientists believe gave the Troodon very good vision, particularly for night hunting.

Here is what you do:

Push the small end of one ice-cream spoon into the side of the Styrofoam ball. Push the end of the second spoon in just below the first spoon to form a flat bill, like a duck's. Press a marble into the ball on each side of the head, just above the mouth. To be sure the marbles stay in place, put a small piece of masking tape in each eye hole and one on the back of each marble. Now glue the eyes in the eye holes.

Push the stick or dowel into the bottom of the head. Cover the head and mouth with aluminum foil, peeling it away around the eyes. Bunch foil around the top part of the stick to shape a body for the Troodon puppet.

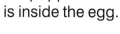 Cut the top half off the oatmeal box. The bottom half of the box will be the Troodon's egg. Cut a jagged edge around the top of the egg.

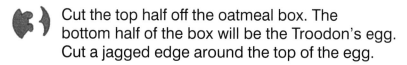 Cut the foot off the sock. Pull the sock over the oatmeal box so that the cut part is at the jagged edge of the egg. Cut a jagged edge around the sock to match the jagged edge of the egg. Poke a hole in the center of the bottom of the oatmeal box. Put the end of the puppet stick through the hole so that the Trodoon is inside the egg.

When you push the stick up, the Troodon peeks out of the egg. Turn the stick left and right so the dinosaur can look around.

Diplodocus Body Puppet

Here is what you need:

10 cardboard toilet-tissue tubes of the same diameter
10-inch (25.4-centimeter) heavy cardboard paper plate
green yarn
cereal-box cardboard
paper scraps in colors of your choice
paint brush and poster paints in colors of your choice
hole punch
scissors
white glue
pinking shears
two rubber bands large enough to fit loosely around your wrist
newspaper to work on

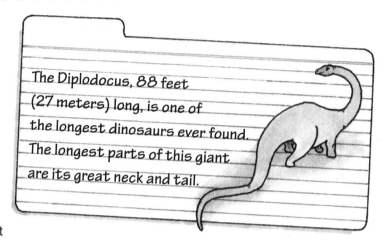

The Diplodocus, 88 feet (27 meters) long, is one of the longest dinosaurs ever found. The longest parts of this giant are its great neck and tail.

Here is what you do:

1) With pinking shears, cut a triangle-shaped slit 3 inches (7.6 centimeters) long on each side of one of the cardboard tubes to form a mouth for the dinosaur. Paint the inside of the tube in the color you want the inside of your dinosaur's mouth to be.

2) From the cereal-box cardboard, cut a triangle-shaped piece that is larger than the opening of one of the cardboard tubes. Punch a hole in the center edge of one side of the triangle.

3) Paint the triangle, the outside of all ten tubes, and the bottom of the plate in the color or colors of your choice. Let all the pieces dry.

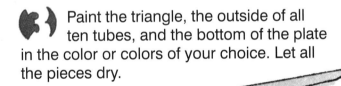

4 The plate will be the dinosaur's body. Punch a hole in the rim. Cut a piece of yarn long enough to string three toilet-paper tubes on. Tie one end of the yarn through the hole in the plate. String three tubes on the yarn. Punch a hole in the back of the tube that makes the dinosaur's head and tie the other end of the yarn through the hole. Trim off any extra yarn.

5 Punch another hole in the rim of the plate, on the opposite side from the first hole. To form the tail, cut a piece of yarn long enough to string four cardboard tubes on. Tie one end of the yarn through the second hole. String the tubes on the yarn, then tie the cardboard triangle to the end of the yarn. Trim off any extra yarn.

6 Cut slits 1 inch (2.5 centimeters) long on each side of the last two tubes. Be sure to cut both slits on the same end of the tube. Slide each tube over the edge of the plate to form the dinosaur's legs. Hold the legs in place with glue.

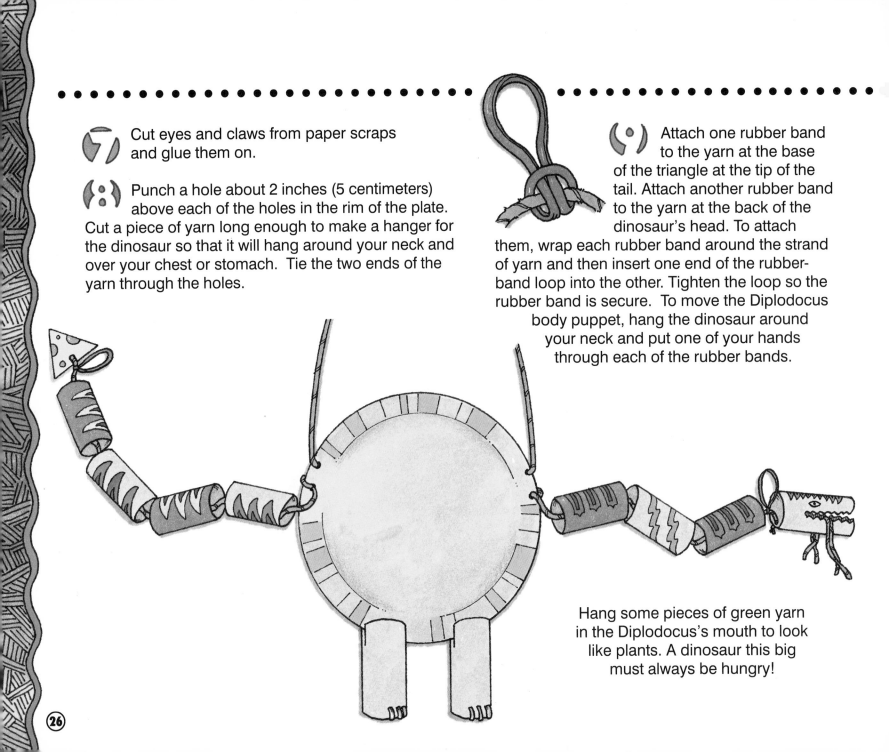

7 Cut eyes and claws from paper scraps and glue them on.

8 Punch a hole about 2 inches (5 centimeters) above each of the holes in the rim of the plate. Cut a piece of yarn long enough to make a hanger for the dinosaur so that it will hang around your neck and over your chest or stomach. Tie the two ends of the yarn through the holes.

9 Attach one rubber band to the yarn at the base of the triangle at the tip of the tail. Attach another rubber band to the yarn at the back of the dinosaur's head. To attach them, wrap each rubber band around the strand of yarn and then insert one end of the rubber-band loop into the other. Tighten the loop so the rubber band is secure. To move the Diplodocus body puppet, hang the dinosaur around your neck and put one of your hands through each of the rubber bands.

Hang some pieces of green yarn in the Diplodocus's mouth to look like plants. A dinosaur this big must always be hungry!

Dinosaur Window Scenes

Here is what you need:

permanent markers in several colors
plastic wrap
dinosaur books or coloring books

Here is what you do:

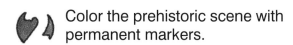

Tear off a large square of plastic wrap. Choose a simple drawing of a dinosaur from a book or coloring book. Place the plastic wrap over the drawing and trace the dinosaur. Find pictures of prehistoric plants, too, and add them to the scene.

Color the prehistoric scene with permanent markers.

The plastic wrap will stick to the window. It will look as if the scene is drawn directly on the glass.

Fill your windows with scenes from the Age of the Dinosaurs.

You can also make your own drawings on the plastic wrap rather than tracing a picture.

Baryonyx Flip Game

Here is what you need:

two cardboard paper-towel tubes
cereal-box cardboard
cardboard egg carton
wooden ice-cream spoon
yarn
aluminum foil
black permanent marker
pinking shears
hole punch
white glue

scissors
masking tape
white and red poster paint
  and other colors of your
  choice
paint brush
cotton swab
newspaper to work on
Styrofoam tray to dry
  your project on

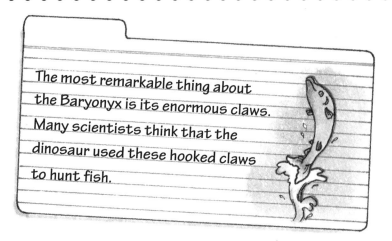

The most remarkable thing about the Baryonyx is its enormous claws. Many scientists think that the dinosaur used these hooked claws to hunt fish.

Here is what you do:

1 With the pinking shears, cut a triangle-shaped wedge, 3 inches (7.6 centimeters) long, out of each side of one end of a tube. This will be the dinosaur's mouth, full of sharp teeth.

2 Cut a slit 6 inches (15 centimeters) long in the other tube. Wrap the two edges of the cut tube around each other to form a cone. Hold the cone shape in place with masking tape. Cut a slit 4 inches (10 centimeters) long in the other end of the tube. Rub glue around the outside of the cut tube and slide it into the first tube, with the cone end out, to form the tail of the dinosaur.

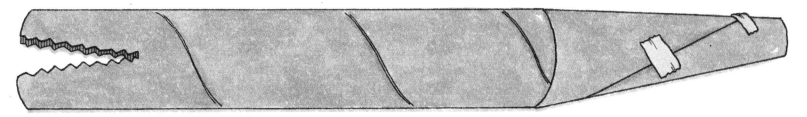

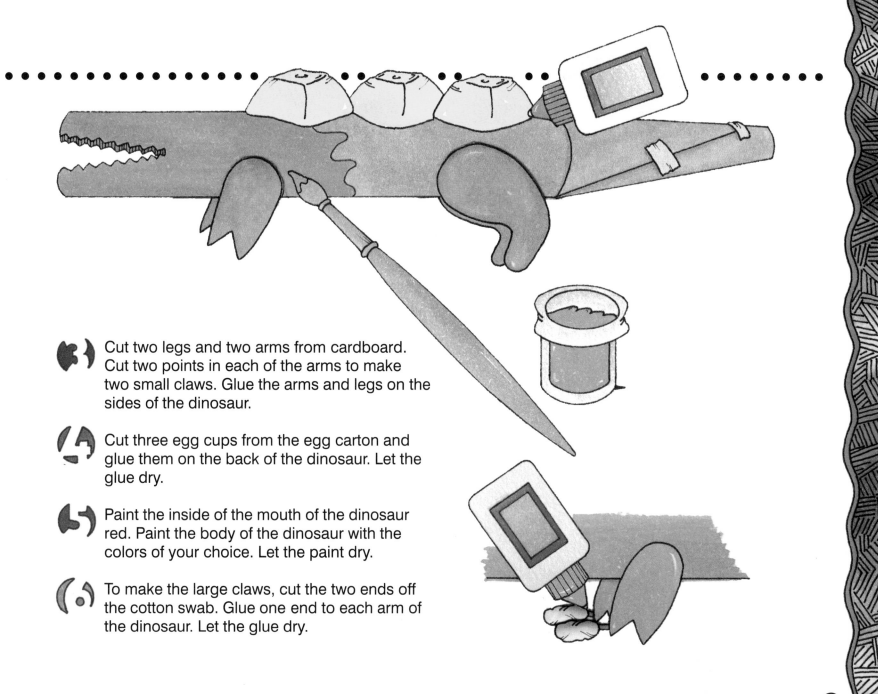

3) Cut two legs and two arms from cardboard. Cut two points in each of the arms to make two small claws. Glue the arms and legs on the sides of the dinosaur.

4) Cut three egg cups from the egg carton and glue them on the back of the dinosaur. Let the glue dry.

5) Paint the inside of the mouth of the dinosaur red. Paint the body of the dinosaur with the colors of your choice. Let the paint dry.

6) To make the large claws, cut the two ends off the cotton swab. Glue one end to each arm of the dinosaur. Let the glue dry.

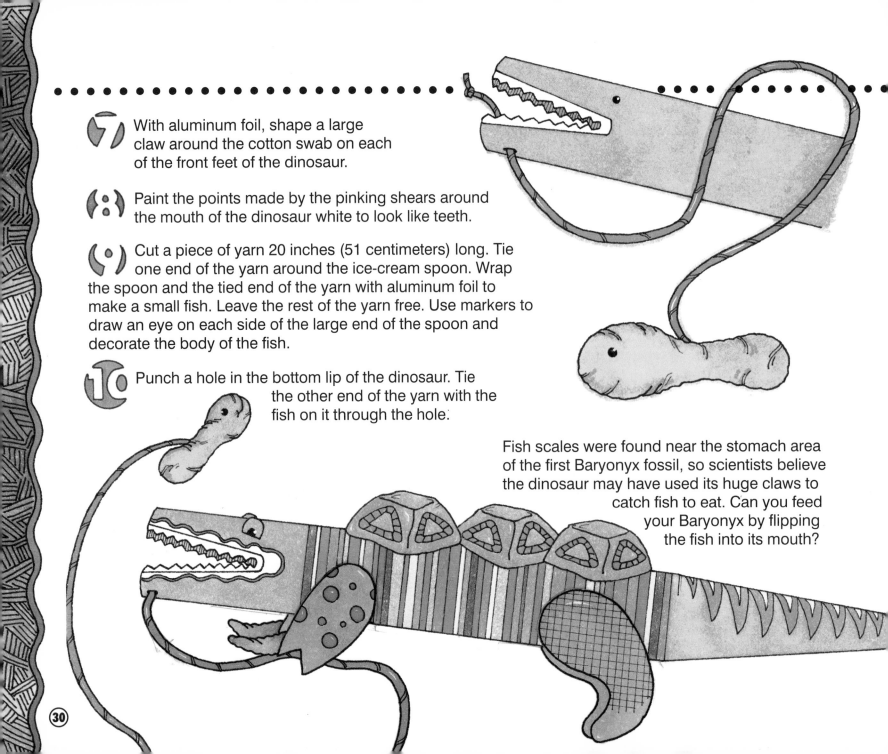

7 With aluminum foil, shape a large claw around the cotton swab on each of the front feet of the dinosaur.

8 Paint the points made by the pinking shears around the mouth of the dinosaur white to look like teeth.

9 Cut a piece of yarn 20 inches (51 centimeters) long. Tie one end of the yarn around the ice-cream spoon. Wrap the spoon and the tied end of the yarn with aluminum foil to make a small fish. Leave the rest of the yarn free. Use markers to draw an eye on each side of the large end of the spoon and decorate the body of the fish.

10 Punch a hole in the bottom lip of the dinosaur. Tie the other end of the yarn with the fish on it through the hole.

Fish scales were found near the stomach area of the first Baryonyx fossil, so scientists believe the dinosaur may have used its huge claws to catch fish to eat. Can you feed your Baryonyx by flipping the fish into its mouth?

Dinosaur in a Cave

Here is what you need:

white construction paper
paint brush and poster paint in a color of your choice
scissors
black marker
paper lunch bag
cellophane tape
Easter grass

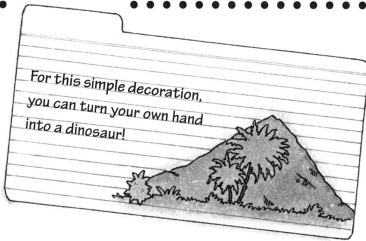

For this simple decoration, you can turn your own hand into a dinosaur!

Here is what you do:

 Paint your hand with poster paint and make a handprint on the white paper. Let the handprint dry.

 Cut the handprint out. The thumb will be the head of the dinosaur. Draw a face with the marker. The fingers will be the legs of the dinosaur. Draw claws on each of the legs.

To make the dinosaur's cave, cut the top half off the lunch bag. On one side of the bag, cut an arched door from the open end almost to the bottom of the bag. Fold over the open end of the bag to the other side and tape it closed.

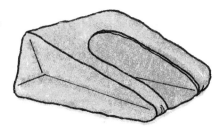

Put the hand dinosaur in the cave with its head sticking out. Tuck some Easter grass in the cave around the dinosaur to make it cozy. If you have a big hand, you may want to make the cave for your dinosaur out of a larger size bag.

Tyrannosaurus Rex Treasure Keeper

Here is what you need:

two plastic gallon-size milk jugs
spray paint in the color of your choice
jumbo white rickrack
masking tape
two paper fasteners
hole punch
scissors
blue glue gel
black marker

Tyrannosaurus Rex was the largest of the meat-eating dinosaurs. Some scientists believe this dinosaur was a quick and fearsome hunter. Others think Tyrannosaurus was a lazy dinosaur who liked an easy meal left by other meat eaters.

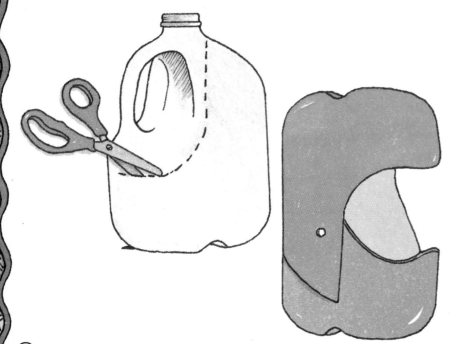

Here is what you do:

Cut around the spout and handle portion of both jugs to remove them. Turn one jug upside-down and slide it over the other jug to form a container with an opening where the handles were cut out. The opening will be the mouth of the dinosaur. Punch a hole through both containers on each side of the mouth. Later, you will hold the two containers together by putting a paper fastener through each of the holes.

Spray both containers with the paint color of your choice. Before you do this, ask a grownup at your house for permission. It's best to do this outdoors, and you may need to have an adult do it for you. Let the containers dry.

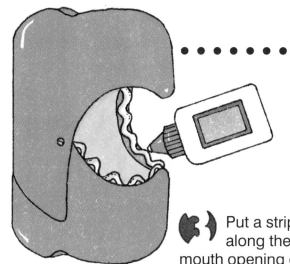

3 Put a strip of masking tape along the inside edge of the mouth opening of each container. This will help the rickrack teeth stick to the plastic. Insert a paper fastener in each of the two holes to hold the containers together. Glue the rickrack along the inside edge of the top and the bottom of the mouth.

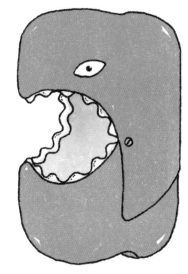

4 Cut eyes from masking tape and stick them on each side of the head above the mouth. Draw a pupil in the middle of each eye with the black marker.

Put Tyrannosaurus Rex on your dresser to keep important stuff in.

Dimetrodon Magnet

Here is what you need:

two wooden ice-cream spoons
craft stick
disposable aluminum pie pan
masking tape
scissors
paintbrush and poster paint in color of your choice
black permanent marker
white glue
piece of sticky-backed magnet
Styrofoam tray to work on

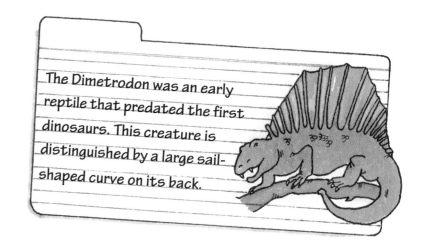

The Dimetrodon was an early reptile that predated the first dinosaurs. This creature is distinguished by a large sail-shaped curve on its back.

Here is what you do:

 The two ice-cream spoons will form the body of the Dimetrodon. The large ends of the spoons should be the dinosaur's head. To make the Dimetrodon's legs, cut a piece about 1 inch (2.5 centimeters) long from each end of the craft stick. Glue the stick legs, rounded ends down, to one of the spoons. Let the glue dry.

Paint both halves of the body, including the legs, and let them dry.

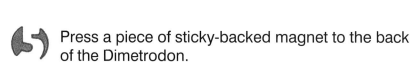 Draw a face and claws on the reptile with the black marker.

Cut a semicircle 2 inches (5 centimeters) wide from the ripply edge of the pie tin to make the sail-shaped curve. Cover both sides of the straight edge of the sail with masking tape and then cover the tape with glue. (Glue won't stick to aluminum, but it will stick to masking tape.) Glue the sail to the back of one of the painted spoons. Then glue on the second wooden spoon to form the other half of the body. Let the glue dry.

Press a piece of sticky-backed magnet to the back of the Dimetrodon.

Stick this prehistoric favorite on your refrigerator for everyone to admire.

Pterosaur Hat

Here is what you need:

two double sheets of newspaper
stapler and staples
scissors
pinking shears
white, yellow, and black construction paper
paint brush and poster paint
white glue
cereal-box cardboard
newspaper to work on
plastic gallon-size jug to dry hat on

Flying reptiles such as the pterosaur filled the skies in prehistoric times.

Here is what you do:

1 Close one double sheet of newspaper and fold the sheet in half widthwise. Fold in the two top corners so that the edges meet at the center of a triangle. Fold the paper below the triangle in half. Then fold it up again so that it forms a double band at the bottom of the hat. Turn the hat over and do the same thing to make a double band on the other side.

 Staple the ends of each band to hold the folds in place.

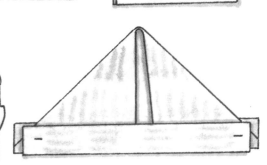

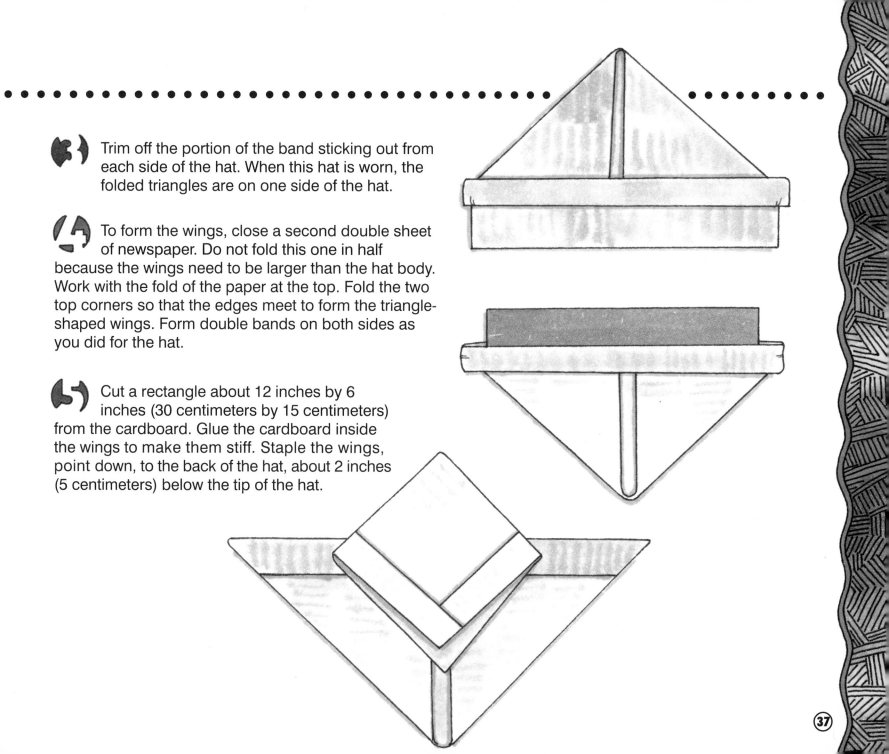

Trim off the portion of the band sticking out from each side of the hat. When this hat is worn, the folded triangles are on one side of the hat.

To form the wings, close a second double sheet of newspaper. Do not fold this one in half because the wings need to be larger than the hat body. Work with the fold of the paper at the top. Fold the two top corners so that the edges meet to form the triangle-shaped wings. Form double bands on both sides as you did for the hat.

Cut a rectangle about 12 inches by 6 inches (30 centimeters by 15 centimeters) from the cardboard. Glue the cardboard inside the wings to make them stiff. Staple the wings, point down, to the back of the hat, about 2 inches (5 centimeters) below the tip of the hat.

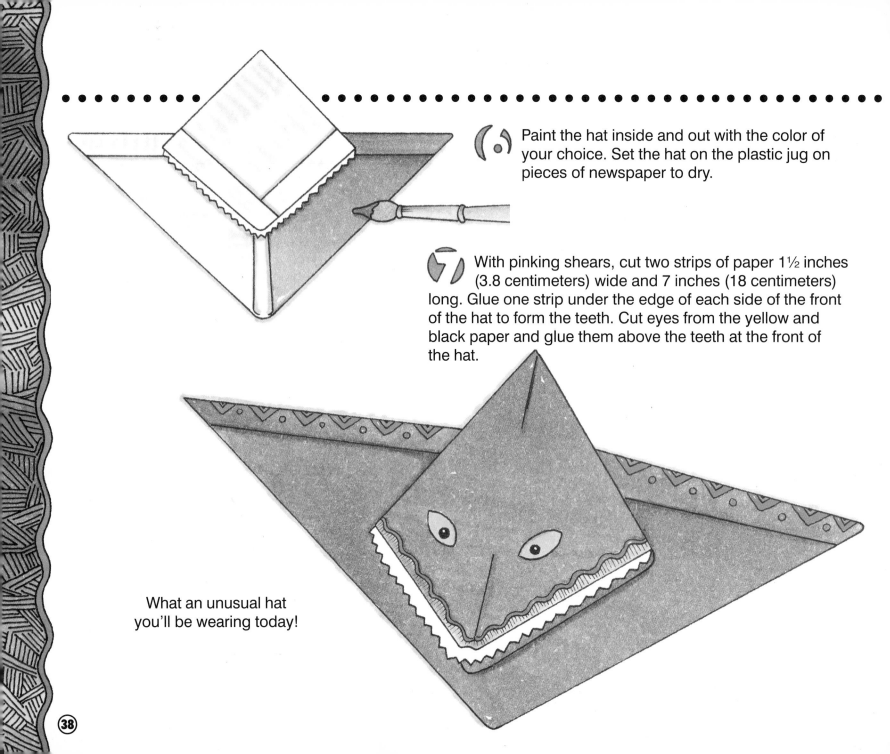

Paint the hat inside and out with the color of your choice. Set the hat on the plastic jug on pieces of newspaper to dry.

With pinking shears, cut two strips of paper 1½ inches (3.8 centimeters) wide and 7 inches (18 centimeters) long. Glue one strip under the edge of each side of the front of the hat to form the teeth. Cut eyes from the yellow and black paper and glue them above the teeth at the front of the hat.

What an unusual hat you'll be wearing today!

Design-a-Dinosaur Art Box

Here is what you need:

large-size cereal box
blue felt, 9 inches by 12 inches
    (23 centimeters by 30 centimeters)
felt scraps in lots of different colors
white glue
scissors

Here is what you do:

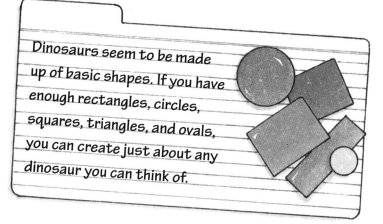

Dinosaurs seem to be made up of basic shapes. If you have enough rectangles, circles, squares, triangles, and ovals, you can create just about any dinosaur you can think of.

Cut the top flaps off the cereal box. Glue the blue felt to the front of the box. You can make the felt-shape dinosaurs on top of this surface.

Cut lots of the basic shapes in different sizes and colors. Working on the blue-felt work surface, arrange the shapes into different kinds of dinosaurs. When you are not using the shapes, you can store them in the cereal box.

As you arrange the shapes, you may decide you need more sizes and colors. Keep adding to your shape collection as you think of what you need for new dinosaur shapes.

Gliding Archaeopteryx

Here is what you need:

toy airplane glider
12-inch (30-centimeter) pipe cleaner
craft feathers in colors of your choice
masking tape
white glue
scissors
black marker

Some scientists believe these ancient birds flew just as well as modern birds do. Others believe that they used their sharp claws to climb trees and their wings to glide, rather than fly, down to the ground.

Here is what you do:

If the glider you are using is made of Styrofoam rather than cardboard or balsa wood, cover the top and sides with strips of masking tape to help the feathers stick.

Cut a 6-inch (15-centimeter) piece of pipe cleaner. Wrap it around the center of the glider behind the wings and let the two ends hang down to form the legs of the bird. Wrap a smaller piece of pipe cleaner around the bottom of each leg to form claws.

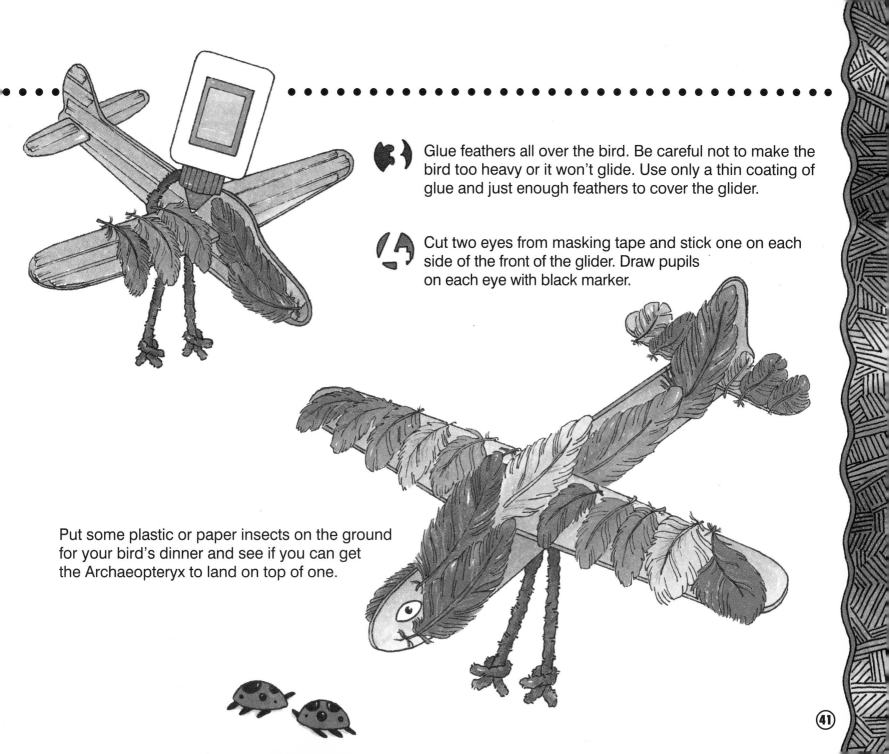

Glue feathers all over the bird. Be careful not to make the bird too heavy or it won't glide. Use only a thin coating of glue and just enough feathers to cover the glider.

Cut two eyes from masking tape and stick one on each side of the front of the glider. Draw pupils on each eye with black marker.

Put some plastic or paper insects on the ground for your bird's dinner and see if you can get the Archaeopteryx to land on top of one.

Plesiosaur Window Decoration

Here is what you need:

plastic egg left over from Easter
aluminum foil
colorful markers
masking tape
black and blue permanent markers
quart-size zip-to-close bag
hole punch
yarn
scissors

The Plesiosaurs were among the many strange-looking reptiles that filled the seas during the Age of the Dinosaurs.

Here is what you do:

Tear off about 7 inches (18 centimeters) of aluminum foil. Wrap the foil around the plastic egg, leaving about 2 inches (5 centimeters) of foil at one end of the egg to form the tail and the rest of the foil at the other end to form a long neck.

Squeeze the foil for the neck and the tail into tight, thin strips. Point the tail slightly downward. Point the neck upward and tip the end forward to shape a head. Squeeze the front of the head into a point.

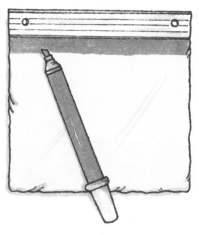

With the black marker, draw eyes on the head and flipper-like arms and legs on each side of the egg body.

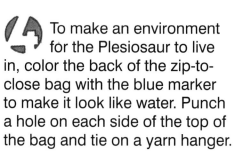

To make an environment for the Plesiosaur to live in, color the back of the zip-to-close bag with the blue marker to make it look like water. Punch a hole on each side of the top of the bag and tie on a yarn hanger.

Draw some tiny fish on masking tape. Color the fish and cut them out. Stick the fish in the bag for the Plesiosaur to eat for dinner.

Put the Plesiosaur in the bag and hang it in a sunny window.

Stones-in-the-Stomach Dinosaur Game

Here is what you need:

small coffee can
four cardboard paper-towel tubes
brown construction paper
black marker
paint brush and poster paints in two colors
scissors
cellophane tape
scrap paper
white glue
four stones small enough to fit in the tubes
newspaper to work on

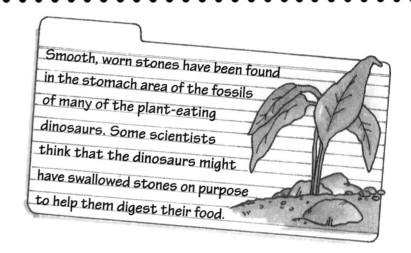

Smooth, worn stones have been found in the stomach area of the fossils of many of the plant-eating dinosaurs. Some scientists think that the dinosaurs might have swallowed stones on purpose to help them digest their food.

Here is what you do:

Cut a piece, 2 inches to 3 inches (5 centimeters to 8 centimeters) long, off the end of each tube. Make each piece a different length so that the height of each dinosaur will be slightly different.

Cut a 1-inch (2.5-centimeter) slit in each of the four small pieces of tube. To make a dinosaur, overlap the two cut edges of each tube, rub glue around the overlap, and push that end of the short tube into the longer tube at a slight angle. Now you have an open-mouthed dinosaur head on a long neck. Make four of these dinosaurs.

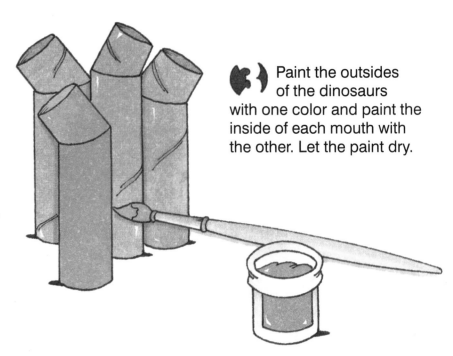

Paint the outsides of the dinosaurs with one color and paint the inside of each mouth with the other. Let the paint dry.

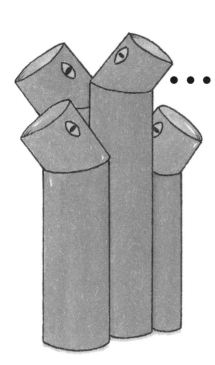

Cut two eyes for each dinosaur out of scrap paper. Glue the eyes on and draw pupils in them with the black marker.

Cover the coffee can with brown paper. Tape it in place.

Put the four dinosaurs in the can with the mouths facing outward. Draw a different number on each dinosaur. Every time you toss a stone into the mouth of one of the dinosaurs, add the number written on that dinosaur to your score.

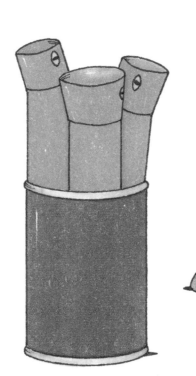

See how many stones you can feed the dinosaurs, or play this game with a friend.

Dinosaur Feet

Here is what you need:

four large brown grocery bags
newspaper for stuffing
four large white Styrofoam trays
masking tape
white glue
scissors

Get together with your friends to make these giant dinosaur feet.

Here is what you do:

1. Stuff a grocery bag loosely with crumpled newspaper. Slide a second bag over the opening of the stuffed bag. Pull the top bag all the way down over the stuffed one.

2. About 3 inches (7.6 centimeters) up from the bottom of the top bag, cut a hole 4 inches (10 centimeters) wide. Fold masking tape around the cut edge of the opening. This will help to keep the hole from tearing while you're wearing the foot.

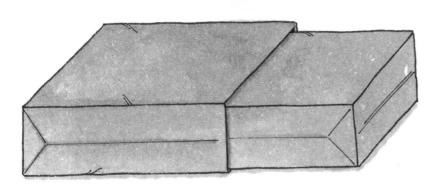

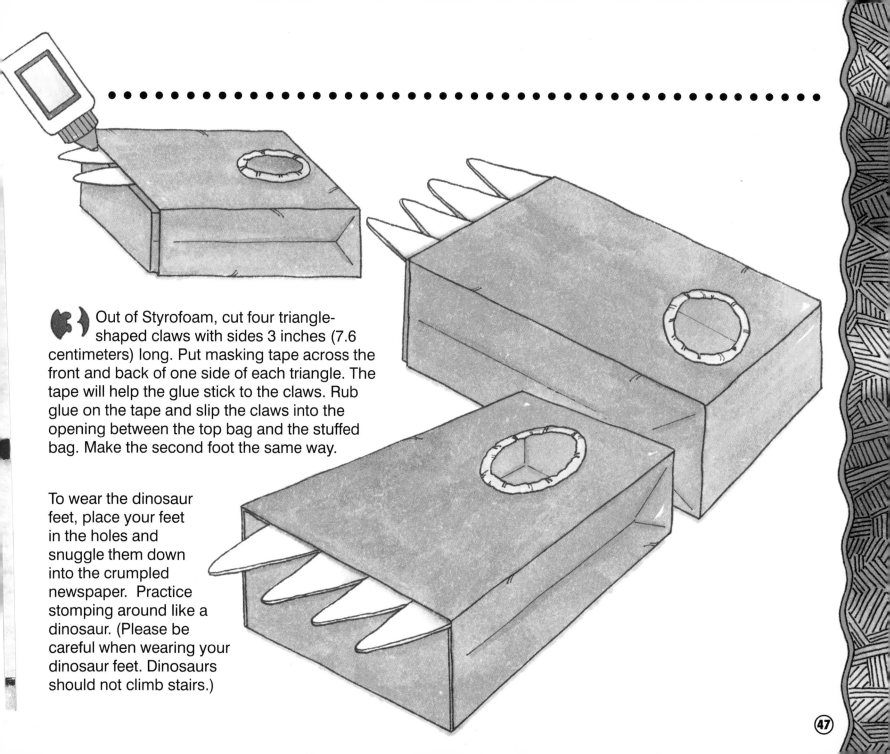

Out of Styrofoam, cut four triangle-shaped claws with sides 3 inches (7.6 centimeters) long. Put masking tape across the front and back of one side of each triangle. The tape will help the glue stick to the claws. Rub glue on the tape and slip the claws into the opening between the top bag and the stuffed bag. Make the second foot the same way.

To wear the dinosaur feet, place your feet in the holes and snuggle them down into the crumpled newspaper. Practice stomping around like a dinosaur. (Please be careful when wearing your dinosaur feet. Dinosaurs should not climb stairs.)

About the author and illustrator

Twenty years as a teacher and director of nursery school programs have given Kathy Ross extensive experience in guiding young children through crafts projects. She lives in Oneida, New York.

Sharon Lane Holm won awards for her work in advertising design before shifting her concentration to children's books. Her illustrations have added zest to books for both the trade and educational markets. She lives in New Fairfield, Connecticut.

Kathy Ross and Sharon Lane Holm have also created the popular eight-book series Holiday Crafts for Kids, published by The Millbrook Press.

DATE			